# HERITAGE

# MOTORCYCLES

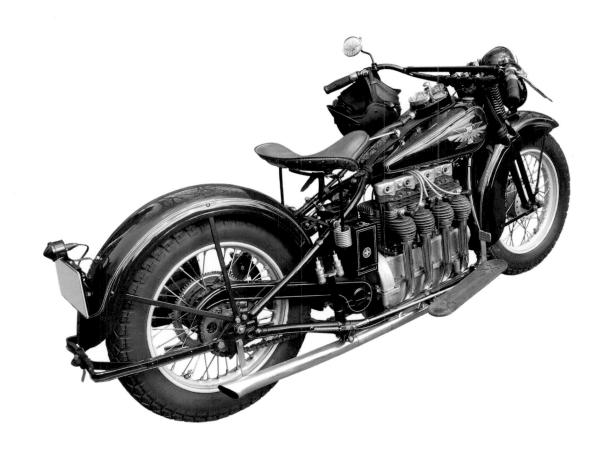

# HERITAGE

# MOTORCYCLES

## Patrick Hook

COMPENDIUM

This edition published in 2008 by

**COMPENDIUM**

ISBN: 978-1-906347-58-1

2008 by Compendium Publishing Ltd.
43 Frith Street, London W1D 4SA,
United Kingdom

Cataloging-in-publication data is available from
the Library of Congress.

Designer: Dave Ball
Color reproduction: Anorax Imaging Ltd
Printed and bound in China

### Acknowledgments
I would especially like to thank my friend Ed
Riggins for all his time and efforts in helping me
source the images for this book. I am also
indebted to his staff members Kevin Convertito
and Randy Dodson, as well as his good friend
Jim Service. Most of all, however, I would like to
thank the Perkins family, with special mention to
James and Tom Perkins for their kind permission
to use the wonderful historical images from their
personal photo album. I only wish we had the
space to feature more of them! Other major
contributors include: The Library of Congress,
Prints and Photographs Division, an old friend
with whom I have worked many times before—
Simon Clay—and Corbis: thanks to Magnus
Jigstedt and Toby Hopkins. Further images were
supplied by: Georg Dieter, Brian Ducharme,
Caio Cassoli, Daniel Hohlfeld, Henry Azuil,
Allyson Correia, Keith Syvinski, Jason
Boutsayaphat, Troy Sherk and Joel Terrell.

PAGE 1: Excelsior-Henderson 4-cylinder. *Georg Dieter*

PAGES 2–3: V-Rod engine detail. *Henry Azuil*

RIGHT: 1950s Indian Chief. *Simon Clay*

# CONTENTS

# INTRODUCTION

**ABOVE:** Like many other manufacturers of the time, Excelsior were keen to exploit the marketing aspects of achieving significant records. Here the winner of a San Francisco to Chicago endurance event is congratulated for his efforts. *Dudley Perkins Family*

**RIGHT:** Board track racing was one of the most popular forms of motor sport in the 1910-1920 era. Here, the rider of an early Indian racer poses with his trusty mount. *Dudley Perkins Family*

**FAR RIGHT:** Charles Hutchison was an actor and director whose film career lasted from 1914 until 1944. He was well-known for his tough guy roles, and performed all his own stunts, including jumping over a broken bridge on a motorcycle, a feat that is promoted in the images seen here. *Dudley Perkins Family*

LEFT: The engine in the 1915 Model 11-K was so well engineered that it made hardly any mechanical noise—before long, this factor, combined with its color scheme, led to it being widely known as "The Silent Gray Fellow." *Randy Dodson/Dudley Perkins Family*

BELOW: It is difficult to know exactly what is going on in this photograph—a velocipede rider appears to be in the middle of being issued with some form of ticket by a motorcycle cop. 1921. *Library of Congress*

BELOW RIGHT: Dudley Perkins, the founder of the famous Harley-Davidson dealership in San Francisco, was a very accomplished competitor in a wide variety of motorcycle sport. Here he poses with yet another trophy after a successful event. *Dudley Perkins Family*

RIGHT: This poster promoting the Indian Motocycle (sit) Company was originally captioned:

*"Since the creation of the Indian Motorcycle the Indian Factory has been the greatest of its kind in the world. The tremendous facilities of this factory are laid out over 12 acres of floor space-nothing short of an actual visit will enable you to visualize the manufacture of today's Indian motorcycles. In making a tour of the 35 departments of the factory, a person would walk a distance of 7 miles. The row upon row of machinery, if placed end to end, would alone stretch out over 1½ miles. Indian leadership has been maintained thru the years by that manufacturing expertness which finds its outlet in making each new Indian better than the best Indian which has gone before it.—When you ride on an Indian, you ride on the Best."* © Lake County Museum/Corbis

throughout the 1920s, but times were still hard, a matter made much worse by the stock market crash in the late 1920s, and the onset of the Great Depression in the early 1930s. It was clear to all that things were going to get worse before they got better, and as a consequence, the owner of the Excelsior-Henderson company decided to cease trading in 1931. This left just Harley-Davidson and Indian, and both undertook desperate measures in order to cut costs enough to make their machines more affordable. This was done by lowering specifications in many areas, such as reducing the amount of chrome plating and making the paint schemes simpler.

In the run-up to WWII, the U.S. military ordered large numbers of bikes from both manufacturers. While Harley-Davidson did very well out of these contracts, producing over 90,000 bikes for military use, Indian struggled to make a profit, and by the end of the war was in deep financial trouble. By the early 1950s, production of both the Indian Scout and Chief had ceased, and the company was relying on the importation of cheap foreign products which it then sold under its own name. After more than sixty years trading, it finally closed down in 1962.

With the demise of Indian Motorcycles, Harley-Davidson was left to take on the tide of foreign imports. At first, these were mostly from Europe, with Britain, Germany and Italy being the predominant suppliers. It was not long, however, before the Japanese moved in on the U.S.—after all, it represented the world's largest market. Although their products were not taken seriously initially, what began as a trickle of imports soon turned into an enormous flood. In 1964, a new American-made motorcycle appeared—this was called the Hodaka, and was produced in Oregon by a U.S.-Japanese company.

In spite of the enormous amount of ill-feeling caused by Japan's behavior

**ABOVE:** Although the main roads through towns and cities were generally of a reasonable standard, those found elsewhere were often in an appalling state—consequently, wide handlebars were fitted in order to provide greater control. 1922 July 20. *Library of Congress*

**ABOVE MIDDLE:** Here, members of the Perkins family are about to set off with two sidecar-equipped Harley-Davidsons, bearing a large consignment of presents in the run-up to Christmas, 1921. *Dudley Perkins Family*

**ABOVE RIGHT:** President Calvin Coolidge poses next to a sidecar-equipped motorcycle in front of the White House. He was United States President from 1923–1929. This photo was taken on 6/6/24. *Library of Congress*

**RIGHT:** Seven Harleys lined up outside a motorcycle dealership. It is interesting to note that three of them—along with the one in the window, are not V-twins, but "fore and aft" horizontally-opposed flat twins. *Library of Congress*

**RIGHT:** The 4-cylinder design of this Excelsior-Henderson motorcycle was originally developed by William and Tom Henderson who founded their own company in 1911. In 1917, however, they sold it to the manufacturer of the Excelsior brand, and from then on a large red cross was added to the logo. *Georg Dieter*

**OPPOSITE PAGE:** The Indian Ace Motorcycle—aimed squarely at the luxury end of the market, came about as the result of the company buying out the Ace Motor Corporation in 1927. This unrestored example bears serial number 001. *Markus Cuff/ 42-15996108 Corbis*

ABOVE: These days, William G. Davidson, is better known to Harley enthusiasts as "Willie G." The grandson of William A. Davidson, one of the founders of the Harley-Davidson Motor Company, he is seen here after winning a 1952 endurance race. February 24, 1952. *Bettmann/Corbis U2106948*

RIGHT: The "45," as it became known was so-named because its capacity was 45ci (750cc). It was first produced in 1929, and amazingly, manufacture continued in one form or another until 1974. This immaculate Harley-Davidson WL45 was restored by ex-racer and engineer Jack Christianson. *Randy Dodson/Dudley Perkins Family*

during the war, the far-eastern machines became popular almost overnight. This was because they were cheap, efficient, reliable, and to a certain extent, disposable. In the first few years of this unexpected invasion, Harley-Davidson was extremely fortunate that the Japanese only made small capacity bikes, but this situation did not last, and before long its sales had begun to plummet. Very few of Harley-Davidson's die-hard customers would have even considered purchasing a Japanese motorcycle—a situation that is still true to this day. The problem for the factory, however, was that it did not make its money out of the out-and-out enthusiast, who only represented a small fraction of the total market. The real profit was to be found in mass sales, and by the mid-1960s, most were going to the Japanese and Europeans. It was not long before the Harley-Davidson company was in serious financial trouble, and in 1969, it was bought by American Machine & Foundry (AMF).

With the purchase by AMF came a series of harsh changes-large numbers of employees were made redundant, and production methods were changed to cut costs. It was quite clear to outsiders that AMF's management did not understand the motorcycle business, and that it was out of touch with its customer base. This resulted in many of the workforce going on strike, and the quality of the machines they made went steeply downhill. This was in stark contrast to the Japanese motorcycles the company had to compete with, which continued to improve year on year. For the first time, Harleys gained a reputation for unreliability, and things spiralled downwards for many years.

In 1981, things changed beyond all recognition at Harley-Davidson when a management buy-out succeeded in wresting control away from AMF. The good times returned, and a series of sweeping changes were made. Unlike the

**LEFT:** This photo shows a motorcycle gathering at Venice, California c1910. *Library of Congress*

**LEFT:** This photo shows the members of the Los Angeles Motorcycle Club at Venice, California somewhere around the year 1911. It was clearly a popular and well-supported group, as the crowd with them is enormous. *Library of Congress*

**LEFT:** This photo shows the members of the Butte Motorcycle Club somewhere around the year 1914. The machines they own are a diverse selection, ranging from lightweight solos to heavyweight sidecar outfits. *Library of Congress*

LEFT: Back when there were few vehicles on the roads, this may have been considered a safe way to travel—it is hard to imagine such a scene being acceptable these days though! 1928 or 1929. *Library of Congress*

ABOVE: Many Harley events draw riders from hundreds, if not thousands of miles away. Here a town has been taken over by large numbers of well-heeled enthusiasts. *Brian Ducharme*

RIGHT: Harleys come in all manner of shapes and sizes—seen here they vary from a Shovelhead custom at one end, to an XLCR Sportster at the other. *Simon Clay*

ones made when AMF bought the company, these were aimed at improving the quality of the machines they produced. Once again, the technical alterations were guided by what the customer wanted, rather than by what the accountants dictated. This was largely led by Willie G. Davidson, grandson of William A. Davidson, a keen motorcycle enthusiast who regularly rode long distances and attended biker events. These changes resulted in an immediate turn-around in sales, something that was considerably helped when the government imposed a large import tax on all bikes over 700cc. In 1984, the first Evolution big-twin engine was introduced—this replaced the ageing Shovelhead, and was an immediate success. Two years later, the Sportster range got its own smaller version, and by 1990, the Harley-Davidson Motor Company had regained the top spot for big bike sales.

Since then, the company has produced two new powerplants, with the first of these being the twin-cam 88 motor. This appeared in 1999, with the extra cam being added to improve the pushrod geometry, something which had been compromised ever since the first overhead valve big-twin was designed more than sixty years before. With ever-tightening noise emission regulations and the requirement for increased engine efficiency, the change was long overdue. The other new engine design arose out of the VR1000 superbike project-named the VRSC, it appeared in the V-Rod in 2001. All the bikes in the Harley product range continue to be updated with new or revamped models appearing on a season by season basis.

**RIGHT:** Harleys are popular the world over—here a line of them can be seen basking in the sun at the Guarujá beach, in Brazil. *Caio Cassoli*

**LEFT:** This engine was produced by Paul Funk, and is known as the Perfect Twin Project, or "PTP" for short. It is based on the Evolution, but has been extensively modified in the search for better performance. *Paul Funk*

**ABOVE:** Star of the film *Easy Rider* was a Harley known as Captain America—this bike, with its Stars and Stripes paintjob, fishtail pipes, and extended front end, was built as a homage to the original. *Simon Clay*

# THE BIG TWINS

RIGHT: The F-Head engine earned the
Harley-Davidson companies many
trophies in its time, including a record-
breaking 100 miles covered at a speed of
89.11mph. This took place on a board
track in Chicago in September, 1915.
*Randy Dodson/Dudley Perkins Family*

# THE BIG TWINS

## HARLEY-DAVIDSON BIG TWINS

The first Harley-Davidson V-twin was produced in 1909; it had an engine capacity of 1000cc, and made 7 horsepower. It proved to be a successful format, and this bike's descendants are still being manufactured today. The factory produced several different 45 degree V-twin designs over the years, with the first long line being known as the JD or F-Head. Production of this inlet over exhaust engine ran from 1914-29. After this came a series of engines, each of which was been given a nickname based on the appearance of the cylinder heads. The flathead engines, for example, were so named because they had side-valves, and the heads were therefore flat. Those on the Knucklehead, however, had overhead valves, and the shape of the rocker covers alluded to the two end knuckles on a fist. Perhaps the most easily recognised engine is the Panhead-the rocker covers on this look like upside-down saucepans. Explaining just how the cylinder head on a Shovelhead looks like a shovel is less straightforward, however, the rectangular form of the Evolution's top-end easily explains why it is sometimes called the Blockhead.

## THE FLATHEAD

The name Flathead was applied to a range of side-valve engines which were manufactured between 1929 and 1974. Most had a capacity of 45ci (750cc) and were

LEFT: When the 74ci (1200cc) side-valve Flathead VL was released in 1930, it had a series of teething problems. These were addressed when the VLD—as seen here— was introduced in 1934. *Randy Dodson/Dudley Perkins Family*

fitted to such utility models as the WLA and the Servi-Car. This was a very successful design, and it was used to power tens of thousands of machines over the years. Larger versions, designated as the VL, were also made-these measured 74ci (1200cc), but in spite of the extra capacity, the ownership experience proved to be a major disappointment for a lot of customers. The main reason for this was the bikes' incredible weight—at 530 lbs., they were far too heavy for the modest power outputs they delivered. To make matters worse, they vibrated terribly above 50mph, and suffered from a range of mechanical problems, including potentially terminal issues such as crankshaft failures and frame breakages. Many owners, as well as significant numbers of dealers, were so upset by the problems they'd experienced that they deserted the Harley-Davidson brand altogether and moved over to the Indian product range. In the end the factory had to rush through a major redesign in order to sort out the problems and prevent the loss of any more customers.

**LEFT:** The Flathead 45 was first introduced in 1929 as the Model D—this was a direct competitor to the Indian 101 Scout and Excelsior Super X. It proved to be such a success that it stayed in production in one form or another until 1973. During this time it powered solos, sidecars, and the ubiquitous Servi-Car. *Randy Dodson/Dudley Perkins Family*

BELOW: In 1932, the Model D 45 Flathead was updated and released as the Model R. Although the two engines both displaced the same capacity, there were many significant differences between them, including such things as the crankcases, timing case, and oil pump. *Randy Dodson/Dudley Perkins Family*

ABOVE AND PAGES 26–27: Before the advent of foot-change transmissions, gear control was performed using a hand-change mechanism which was mounted on the side of the gas tank, as seen here. *Randy Dodson/Dudley Perkins Family*

LEFT: The Knucklehead engine was so-named because of the supposed similarity between the shapes of the rocker covers and the knuckles on a fist. *Daniel Hohlfeld*

BELOW: The 40bhp Knucklehead engine first appeared in 1936, and proved to be the first in a long line of big-twin engines that are still being made today. *Randy Dodson/Dudley Perkins Family*

## THE KNUCKLEHEAD

The overhead valve Knucklehead engine first appeared in 1936, and with 40bhp, it was a lot more powerful than its side-valve predecessors. The first production machines, however, had a series of teething issues that initially marred the design's reputation. For the first time, the 61ci (1000cc) engines had fully re-circulating lubrication—while this was ostensibly a major improvement over the primitive system it replaced, it proved far from trouble-free. The factory tried out several different "fixes," but it was not until an entirely new pump was fitted in 1941, that the problems were finally solved. At first sight, it may seem that this should never have been allowed to happen, however, it must be remembered that all this occurred at a time when the Great Depression had pushed the company to the very brink of bankruptcy. Resources were therefore extremely stretched, and the engineers did the best they could. The last "Knucks" were manufactured in 1947.

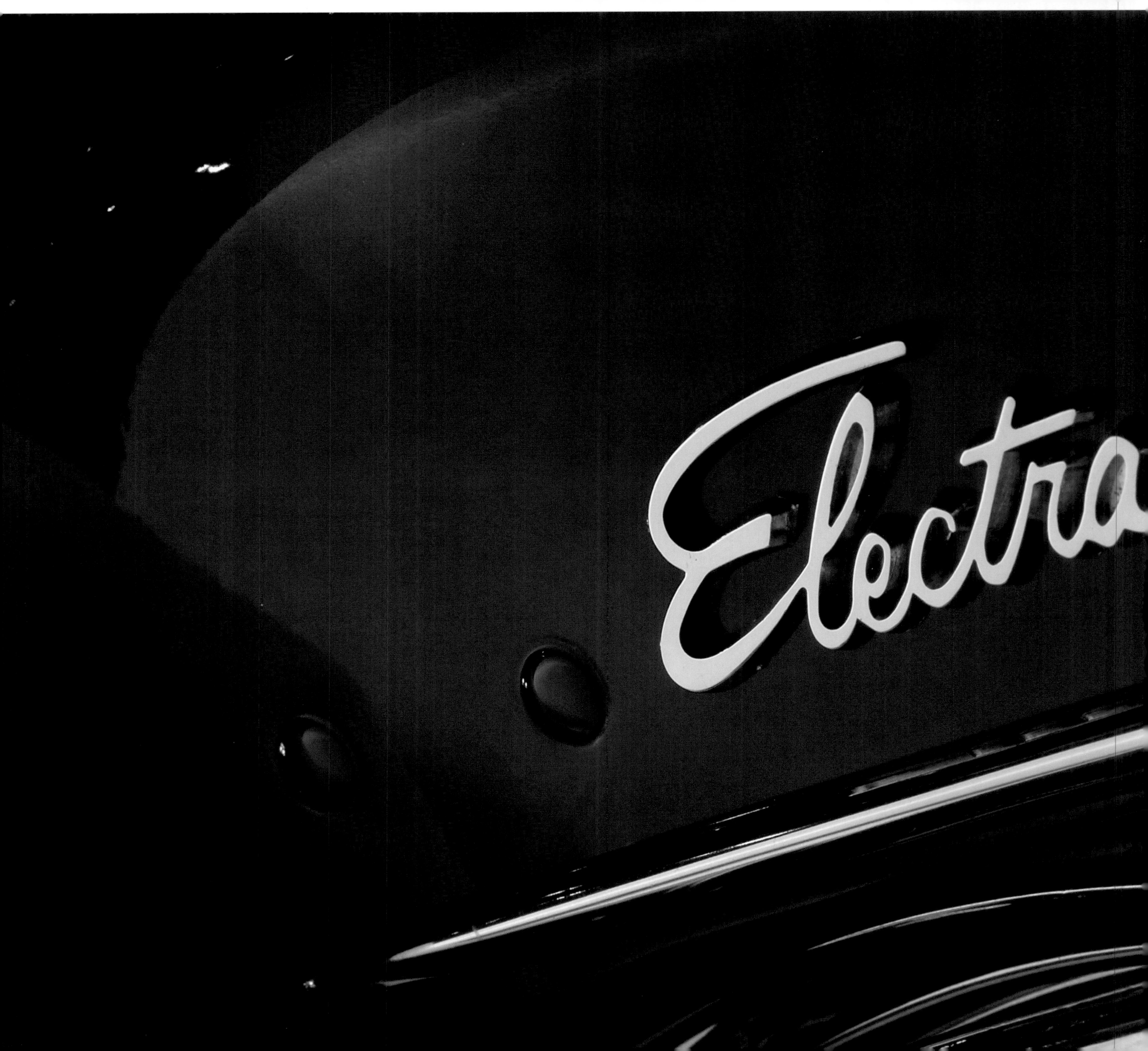
Electra

## THE SHOVELHEAD

The Shovelhead was first released in 1966, first as a 74ci engine, and then later in an 80ci (1340cc) format. Although the production run continued until 1984, thanks to the woes of AMF management, it changed little over this period, and was well out of date by the time the company returned to private ownership. Many people consider the shorter stroke 74's to be the superior engine-they vibrated less, and were thus nicer to ride.

**BELOW AND BELOW RIGHT:** These two Shovelhead chops make no false pretences with glaring paintjobs or fancy metalwork—they are exactly what they seem, with clean lines and an impressive attention to detail. *Simon Clay*

**RIGHT:** The two beautifully-constructed custom Harleys seen here show off the classic lines of the Shovelhead engine well. *Simon Clay*

ABOVE: When AMF took over the Harley-Davidson factory in 1969, standards fell significantly. Die-hard owners were not deterred, however, and soon rebuilt their bikes properly. Seen here is another example of a Shovelhead custom which has been built with a superb attention to detail. *Simon Clay*

ABOVE RIGHT: This Shovelhead lowrider has a rigid rear-end, an open primary and a simple yet effective paintjob. *Simon Clay*

RIGHT: This Shovelhead was not intended to win custom shows but was built by owner Ed Riggins as a practical everyday rider. It therefore has effective front and rear suspension, low bars, a flat track-style seat, short mufflers, and no fancy paint. *Jim Service*

## THE BLOCKHEAD OR EVOLUTION

The Evolution or Blockhead engine replaced the Shovelhead in 1984. Although it remained an air-cooled, 45 degree, V-twin, it was a major step forward. With development assistance from Ricardo Engineering in England, it had been significantly refined, and was more reliable, smoother, produced less pollution, and made more power as well as torque. Most of the changes were to the top-end. Instead of iron cylinders, it featured aluminium castings with cast-in steel liners, and a much improved combustion chamber layout. The rocker covers were split into three so that the upper parts of the engine could be worked on without having to remove it from the frame. This was necessary as the motor was taller than its Shovelhead predecessor. The success of the Evolution engine ensured the survival of the Harley-Davidson Motor Company—had its engineers not delivered such a good design, the factory may well have gone under. Production of the Evo big-twins continued until 1999, when it was replaced by the Twin Cam 88. Its smaller brother, the Evolution Sportster is still being made though.

TOP LEFT: The Evolution engine was a major improvement over the Shovelhead engine. It was more reliable, made more power, and was easier to service. This machine belonged to the late Brandon Lee. *Simon Clay*

TOP RIGHT: Designed to look like it has rigid suspension, the Softail has been produced in many different forms. This lightly-customised model, known as the "Bad Boy," has been fitted with various aftermarket parts such as slash-cut pipes and a sprung seat. *Simon Clay*

BOTTOM LEFT: The Fat Boy, designated as the FLSTF, was designed by Willie G. Davidson. It was created by amalgamating the Softail Custom with the Heritage Softail Classic, and was an immediate sales success. *Simon Clay*

BOTTOM RIGHT: The Low Rider has been sold in various forms for many years—this example is an Evolution-engined model which, like so many Harleys, has had a few minor alterations. *Simon Clay*

## THE TWIN CAM

In 1999, the Evolution engine was replaced by the Twin Cam 88-this was, in effect, a revision of the Evo design, rather than a total re-work. As the name would suggest, there are two main differences—firstly the single camshaft was replaced by twin items, and secondly, the capacity was increased from 80ci (1340cc) to 88ci (1450cc). Twin cams were used in order to reduce engine noise and improve the pushrod geometry. This allowed the engine to run at high revs more easily, whilst helping it to get through ever-stricter noise regulation testing. The new engine provided significantly more power and torque, especially when fitted with larger capacity aftermarket cylinders. Some later versions were fitted with balance shafts, something which met with much derision from many Harley enthusiasts, as this was a common feature of the Japanese "clones."

**ABOVE:** The larger capacity engine fitted to this Twin Cam FXDX produces more torque and horsepower, than that fitted to the Evolution series. At the same time, it makes less engine noise and, thanks to the fitment of balancer shafts, vibrates less. *Simon Clay*

## THE REVOLUTION

In the early 1990s, the Harley-Davidson factory embarked on a project to build a superbike racer. Intended for the World Superbike Championship, it featured a 60 degree engine, twin overhead camshafts, four valves per cylinder, and water cooling. It also had a down-draught intake system, which added considerably to the engine's power output. This heralded one of the most radical changes in design philosophy since the first V-twin Harley was built in 1909. When the finished bike reached the racetrack, however, it failed to compete with its rivals. Sadly, although it delivered the intended performance, the competition had moved on considerably. The engine was certainly fast enough, but the bike suffered from a lack of chassis development, and as a result never became a WSB contender. All these efforts were not in vain, however, and the design was used as the foundation for a new fuel-injected model range which was developed in collaboration with Porsche. Designated as the VRSC, it is also known as the "Revolution," and delivers 115bhp from 69 cubic inches (1130 cc).

The Revolution
**ABOVE:** The water-cooled engine used in the V-Rod was developed from that used in the VR1000 racer. It has a 60 degree bank angle and downdraft intakes. This example has a flame paintjob. *Allyson Correia*

**PAGE 44–45:** The water-cooled engine used in the V-Rod was developed from that used in the VR1000 racer. It has a 60-degree bank angle and downdraft intakes. *Henry Azuil*

**ABOVE:** This example has a flame paintjob. *Allyson Correia*

## INDIAN BIG TWINS

The first Indian V-twin was manufactured in 1907, and its excellent reputation for reliability and performance meant that it was followed by a long line of successors. The layout's inherent strength made it a popular choice with racers and endurance specialists, and the factory were quick to exploit the marketing potential of any notable achievements. One of the most successful designs was known as the "Powerplus"—this had the cylinders arranged at a 42-degree angle, displaced 61ci (1000cc), and was capable of achieving 60mph—a very good figure for the day. It was produced for the first time in 1916, and continued to be manufactured in various variants for many years. It was eventually superseded in 1924, by which time a thriving market for the Indian Scout and Chief had been established. The Scout, with its 37ci (596cc) engine was first introduced in 1920-it was produced in this capacity until 1927, when it was enlarged to 45ci (745cc). In the 1930s, smaller versions known as the Scout Pony, Junior Scout and Thirty-Fifty were also produced. The Indian Chief, which was released in 1922, used an engine that was modelled on the Powerplus. Initially, it displaced 61ci (1000cc), but in 1923, this went up to 73ci (1200cc). Both the Scout and the Chief featured 42-degree V-twin engines, and although they were updated on a regular basis, their overall layout changed little until their production ceased (in the late 1940s and early 1950s, respectively).

LEFT: Indians had an excellent reputation for reliability. This came about because they were very well engineered. *Simon Clay*

**FAR LEFT:** Harleys and Indians ended up looking very similar because they both had to do the same job—provide reliability at an affordable price. This beautifully-restored Indian Chief shows what wonderful machines were around in the 1920s. *Simon Clay*

**CENTER:** Up until the late 1920s, it was common practice to have the valve gear exposed—here the pushrods and rockers are in full view. *Simon Clay*

**LEFT:** Although the first Indian Chiefs made in 1922, were fitted with a 61ci (1000cc) engine, the following year they were enlarged to 73ci (1200cc). By the 1930s, machines such as the one seen here, had benefitted from all manner of detail improvements. *Simon Clay*

BELOW, RIGHT, AND FOLLOWING PAGES:
Although the Harley-Davidson company
managed to make money during WWII, the
Indian factory was in poor financial shape when
the hostilities ended. In a desperate attempt to
resurrect sales, they produced lavish designs,
such as that seen on these pages of this 1950s
Indian Chief. *Simon Clay*

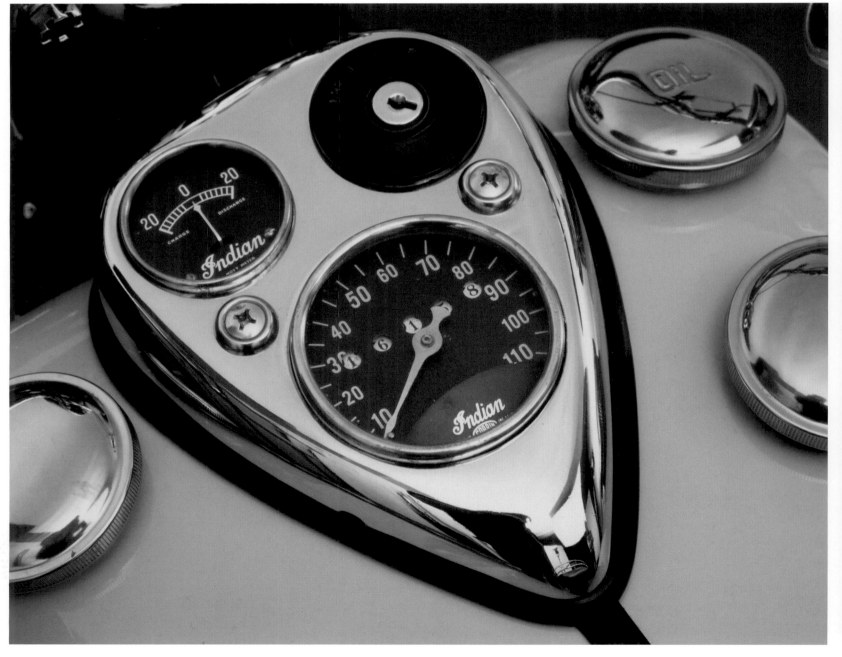

**LEFT:** The original Indian factory went into liquidation in 1962, however, an attempt to revive the name was made in 1999, after the trademark was bought from the owners. Production took place in Gilroy, California, with the bikes using S&S engines; unfortunately the company folded in 2003. *Simon Clay*

**ABOVE:** A close-up of the S&S engine fitted to the Gilroy-manufactured Indian Chief. The company logo was cleverly used in the design of the air cleaner. *Simon Clay*

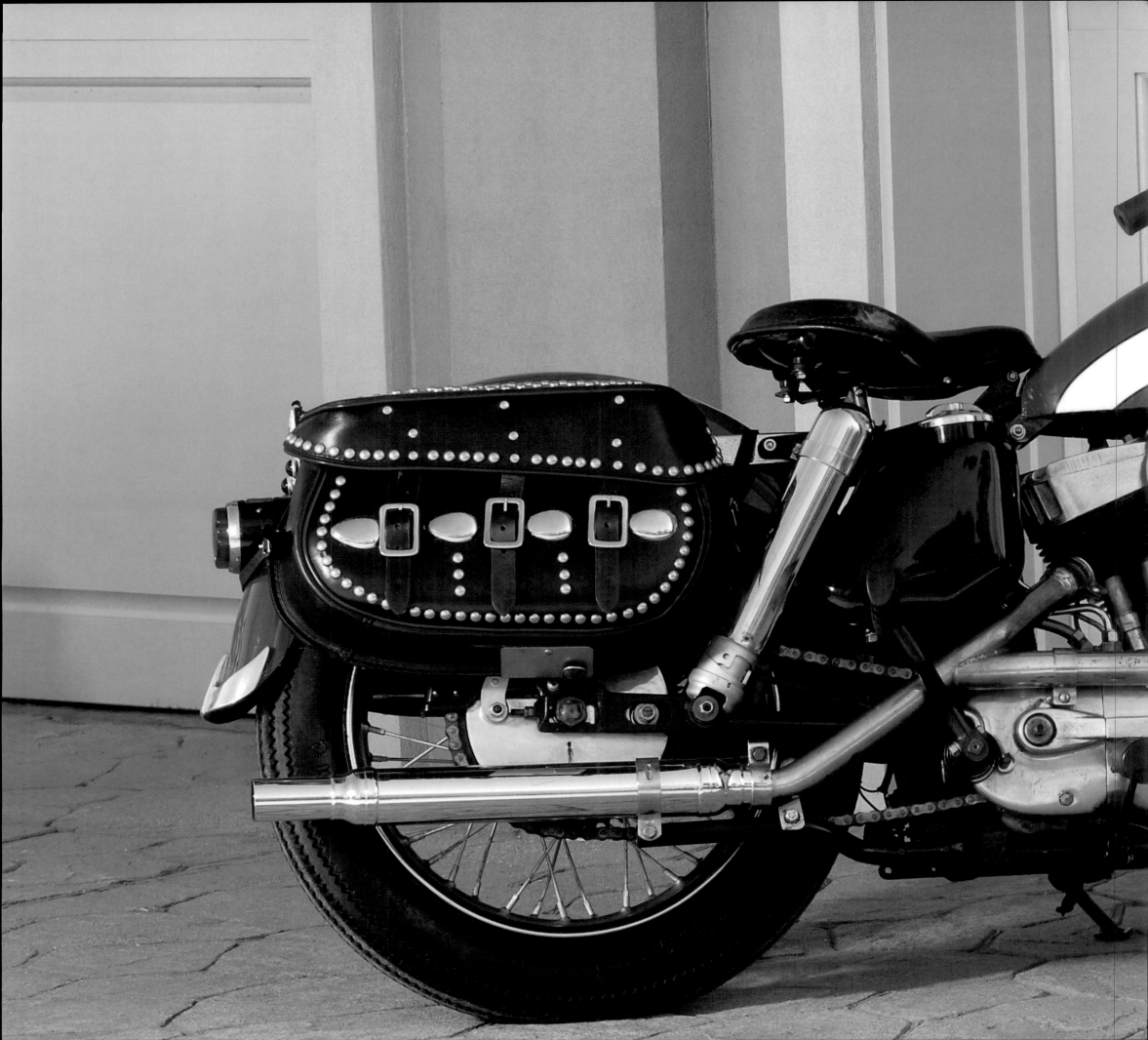

K SERIES &
SPORTSTERS

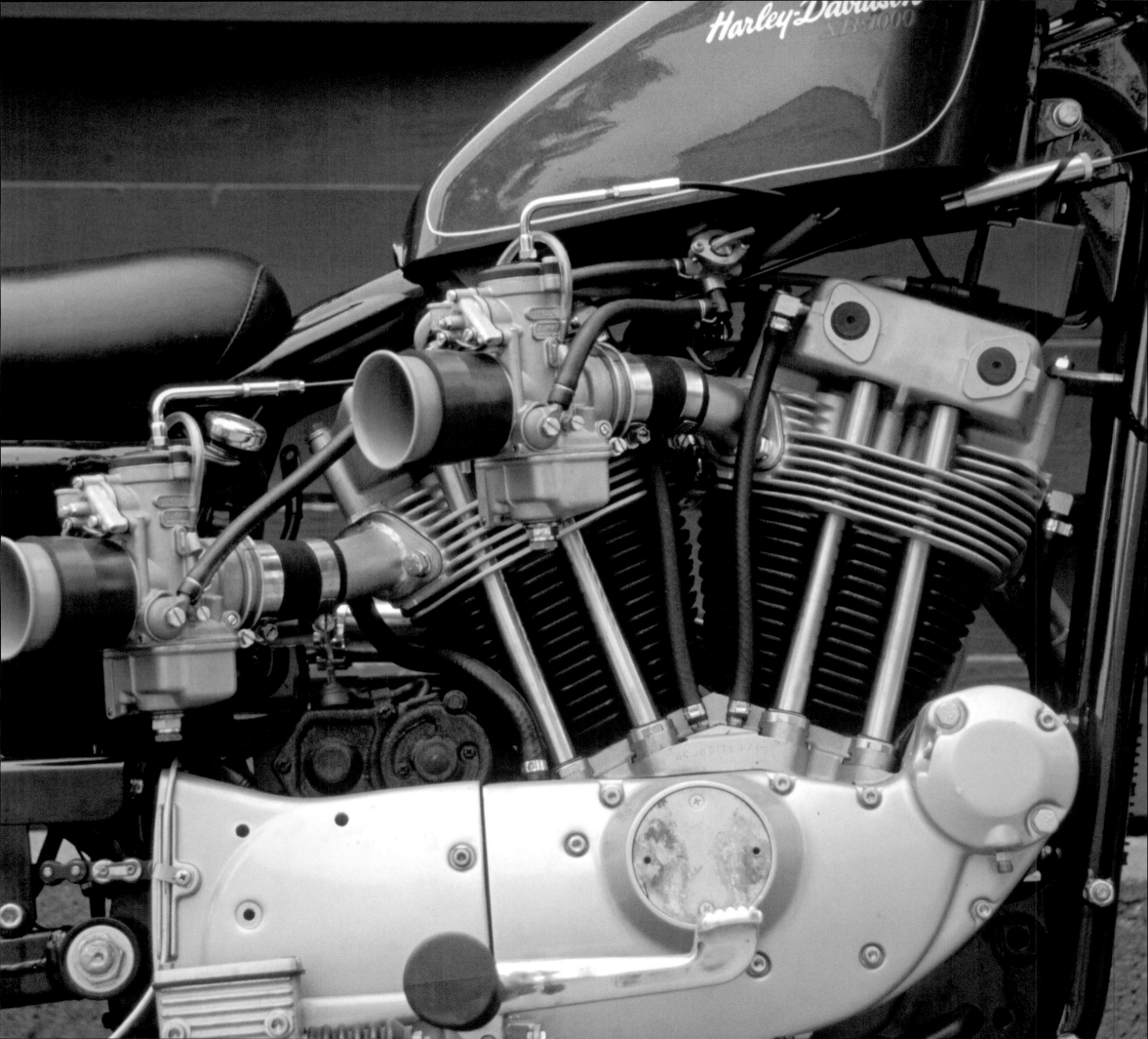

# K SERIES & SPORTSTERS

In 1952, in response to the competition from lighter, faster European bikes, Harley-Davidson produced an entirely new motorcycle with a unit construction engine (where the motor and transmission are integrally-housed). This was known as the "K" Series, and several models were produced in rapid succession. Those designated K and KK had 45ci/750cc engines, whereas the KH and KHK displaced 55ci/883cc. Although these machines were lighter and more nimble than the various Big Twins in the Harley range, they failed to meet the opposition on performance. This was mostly because they still had old-style side-valve engines. In 1957, the factory made up for lost time with the introduction of the overhead valve-engined XL Sportster. This

The 1100cc variant was soon dropped, however, and replaced by a 1200cc version. The Evolution engine was a massive success—it was more reliable, performed better, and was an instant sales hit. Ever since its introduction in 1957, the engine had been rigidly-mounted, however, in 2004, the design was altered to incorporate rubber anti-vibration mountings. Although it made the bike slightly heavier, it reduced rider fatigue over long distances, broadening the model's appeal. In line with all the company's other efforts to improve

proved to be a big hit, and it became the first in a long line of Sportster models-indeed, its descendants are still being produced today, more than fifty years later. Over the first decade the range did not change very much, with most of the alterations being purely cosmetic. Although the engine was enlarged to 1000cc in 1972, few other modifications were made-the most obvious exceptions being the models like the XLCR1000 Café Racer. It was styled by Willie G. Davidson, and just over 3,100 were made during 1977–1979, retailing for $3,595.00. At the time it received a lot of criticism in the press, and did not sell well. Since then, however, its desirability has skyrocketed, and it has become one of the most sought-after models of the modern era.

In 1986, the Sportster range received a major update in the form of the Evolution engine. Initially, this came in two engine capacities—883cc and 1100cc.

efficiency and reduce emissions, the Sportster range was fitted with fuel injection from 2007.

When Eric Buell, an ex-Harley-Davidson engineer and privateer racer decided to set up The Buell Motorcycle Company, he chose to use the Sportster engine as his main powerplant. In 1998, five years after first partnering with him, the Harley factory bought a majority shareholding from him. Several models have used the Sportster engine, including the Firebolt, Lightning, Ulysses, Thunderbolt, and Cyclone. Most of the first ones used the twin-carb XR1000 engine, but when these ran out, the standard 1200 unit was substituted. Since then, many modifications have been made so that they demonstrate very good performance-some models develop over 100bhp, which is a significant amount more than could ever be achieved from a stock Sportster. The handling has also been attended to, with quality suspension components and racetrack-inspired geometry; this can easily be seen in the steep fork angle and short wheelbase. Buell motorcycles have always been characterised by innovative design, with features such as the perimeter disc brakes being most unlike anything seen on other production motorcycles.

LEFT: The XR1000 was produced as the result of one of Willie G's design exercises. It was basically a Sportster with XR-style twin-carb heads. The result was a beautiful machine but it didn't sell particularly well at the time—these days, however, it is highly sought-after by collectors. *Jim Service*

**TOP:** The classic lines of the early Sportsters are still evident in the very latest models made today. *Simon Clay*

**CENTER:** The Sportster is smaller and lighter than the big-twin models, and so is often seen as an easy route to Harley ownership. It has been popular ever since it was first introduced in the 1950s, and still continues to sell well to this day. *Simon Clay*

**ABOVE:** This 1200 Sportster has a very low seat height, and is one of several models that were specifically targeted at women riders. *Simon Clay*

LEFT: Along with its twin-carb heads, the XR1000 also used twin high-level exhausts, just like the XR750 flat track racers it emulated. *Jim Service*

ABOVE: This Sportster-engined Buell has a lightweight steel frame. The massive underslung exhaust silencer is a feature of many of the models produced by this manufacturer. The loud graphics, low handlebars, bikini fairing, and rear-set footpegs leave little doubt that this bike was built for performance. *Simon Clay*

RACERS

ABOVE: Everyone loves to be associated with a
winner, and this team are rightly proud of their
rider's achievements. *Dudley Perkins Family*

**ABOVE:** Here, a group of dirt track racers gather together before an event for a photograph to demonstrate their camaraderie. *Dudley Perkins Family*

**LEFT:** As a community relations exercise, some police forces put on large shows. At this particular event, a motorcycle race was staged— this photo shows the start. *Library of Congress*

**RIGHT:** A line up of dirt track competitors at the Laurel circuit, Maryland, November 25, 1915. *Library of Congress*

**BELOW:** In the days before motorcycles were fitted with clutches, the competitors in a race needed a push-start. This event took place on Labor Day, 1916 at Benning, Md. *Library of Congress*

**ABOVE:** Ralph Hepburn began racing motorcycles as a teenager, and was one of the top riders for many years. He was tragically killed at the age of 52, while practising for the 1948 Indianapolis 500. *Dudley Perkins Family*

**ABOVE:** Ralph Hepburn at speed—he was a well-known racer of both motorcycles and cars. He broke many national records, and rode for both the Harley-Davidson and Indian factories. *Corbis*

**LEFT:** Judging by the lack of dust, this competitor would appear to be well in the lead. 1922. *Library of Congress*

**BELOW:** One of the problems associated with dirt track racing is that if the surface gets too dry, enormous amounts of dust can be raised. This is not only confusing for the spectators, but also very dangerous for those taking part. This event took place in or near Washington, D.C. c.1920. *Library of Congress*

**ABOVE:** Motorcycle races often formed an important part of country fairs—this photo is of a sidecar race which was held at just such an event on September 5, 1922. Note how there is no barrier separating the spectators from the track. *Library of Congress*

**ABOVE:** A solo race at the same event. *Library of Congress*

**LEFT AND ABOVE:** Hillclimb racing was an enormously popular form of motorcycle sport, as can be seen from the number of spectators at this event. *Dudley Perkins Family*

**BELOW:** The pre-race promotion of this event was rudimentary, but effective. The competitors would each line up at the foot of the hill, and attempt to reach the top without crashing. Some tracks were particularly dangerous, and for good reasons, attracted names such as "The Widowmaker." *Dudley Perkins Family*

**ABOVE AND RIGHT:** Although they may not look very steep from the bottom, a view down the hill shows just how severe the gradient really was. *Dudley Perkins Family*

LEFT: The riders who competed in hillclimbs
had to be both tough and skilled individuals.
*Dudley Perkins Family*

ABOVE: The penalties for failure were severe,
and flipping over backwards was a common
occurrence. *Dudley Perkins Family*

LEFT: Each rider tackled the hill on their own, and those who made it all the way to the top were given a time—the fastest being the winner. *Dudley Perkins Family*

ABOVE: This Excelsior-Henderson hillclimber was fitted with wheelie-bars—these prevented the machine from flipping over backwards. Note the paddles on the rear tyre—these gave a massive increase in grip, but necessitated the fitment of a safety frame. *Dudley Perkins Family*

PAGE 86: The rear tyre on this Indian hillclimber was fitted with short lengths of drive chain in order to provide extra grip. *Dudley Perkins Family*

PAGE 87: Orie Steele—a national hill climbing champion—was said to have won more cups and medals than any other rider. He is seen here posing with his trophies astride an Indian road bike. *Bettmann/Corbis U306656INP*

ABOVE: This lovely 1924 JD Hill Climber from the collection of Clark Roessler was originally built by Tom Sifton. It sits in front of a large photo of Dudley Perkins astride a similar machine. *Randy Dodson/Dudley Perkins Family*

RIGHT: Endurance riding events were very popular—here, three tired competitors pose for the camera after completing a gruelling event. *Dudley Perkins Family*

**ABOVE:** Three competitors in the Firestone Motorcycle Endurance Challenge Trophy Cup pose for the camera on their fore-and-aft Harley-Davidson Model W sport twins. *Dudley Perkins Family*

**LEFT:** Dudley Perkins—"Dud Senior," as he later became known, was a fearless competitor in many forms of motorcycle sport, and was one of the leading riders for many years. He is seen here part-way up a hillclimb track, with every ounce of his being focused on successfully making it to the top. *Dudley Perkins Family*

**RIGHT:** The Firestone Tire and Rubber Company sponsored Motorcycle Endurance Challenge Trophy Cup took place every year, and each manufacturer was allowed to enter one team of three solo machines. This photo shows three successful Harley-Davidson riders with their trophy. *Dudley Perkins Family*

THIS PAGE: In spite of the terrible risks the riders faced, motorcycle racing was still a relatively low-budget affair. Getting the bikes to and from the tracks using makeshift trailers was a long way removed from the vast transporters that are seen today. *Dudley Perkins Family*

LEFT: Dudley Perkins—seen here on the left, was a great sportsman. Long after his own racing career was over, he could still be seen at the tracks giving encouragement and advice to novice riders. When he could no longer walk, he didn't give up, but used a Harley Topper in order to still make his way around the paddock. *Dudley Perkins Family*

ABOVE: This photo of a beautiful vintage Indian flat-tracker shows the steep fork angle that was needed in order to remain in control when pitching and sliding around a loose circuit. *Ed Riggins*

HARLEY
RACERS
Machines and men from flat track, hillclimb,
speedway, motocross and road racing

1957 KR
Roadracer
-from the collection of-
Al Bergstrom
Formerly #98

LEFT: This 1957 Harley-Davidson KR750 Roadracer from the collection of Al Bergstrom was used by Joe Leonard during his extensive racing career, during which time he won the inaugural AMA Grand National Championship Series in 1954. He followed this up with further wins in 1956 and 1957, but retired from bike racing in 1961 to take up car racing. *Randy Dodson/Dudley Perkins Family*

RIGHT: This 1969 KR750 Flat Track Racer from the collection of Al Bergstrom was used by Mark Brelsford during the early part of his six-year career in dirt track competitions. *Randy Dodson/Dudley Perkins Family*

1969 KR

Flat Track Racer

from the collection of

Al Bergstrom

Formerly #67 Mark Brelsford

LEFT: This is the machine that Mark Brelsford used to become the 1972 AMA Grand National Champion. It is a 1972 XR750 Flat Track Racer from the collection of Cary D. Buck. *Randy Dodson/Dudley Perkins Family*

1972 XR750

Flat Track Racer

from the collection of

Cary D Buck

Formerly 1972 AMA #1, Mark Brelsford

**ABOVE:** The XR750 racing engine needs to be set up meticulously if it is to perform at its best—here, the cam timing is in the process of being set up on the workbench. *Jim Service*

**RIGHT:** A late model XR750 Flat Track Racer that was used by Loral Lake Racing in the AMA Grand National Dirt Track Series. *Randy Dodson/Dudley Perkins Family*

RIGHT: Drag racing has always been popular in American motorcycle sport. The Harley-Davidson factory have recently produced a dedicated drag racer known as the Factory V-Rod Destroyer. Here, a number of riders competing in the 2007 AHDRA Race at the Sturgis Dragway can be seen lining up for the start. *Peter Turnley/Corbis 42-19285476*

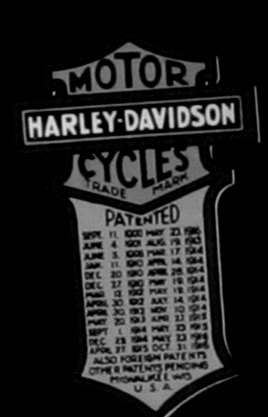

# CUSTOM BIKES

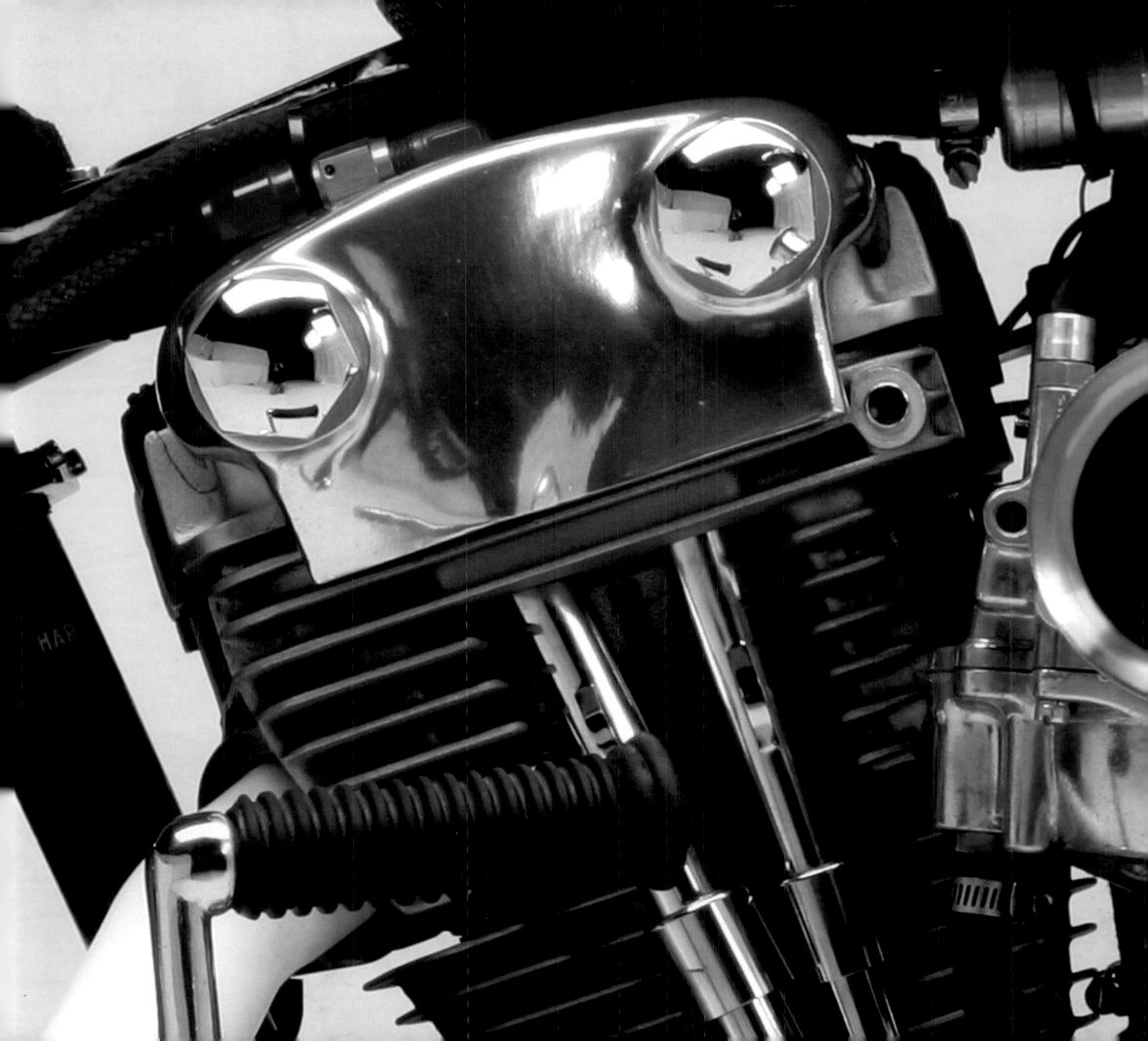

# CUSTOM BIKES

After WWII, a lot of ex-servicemen returning from foreign shores found it hard to go back to working on the farms and homesteads that they grew up on. Instead, many of those who had served with one another in battle, decided to stick together in peacetime too. Often, they formed small bike clubs using military surplus bikes, and went on the road in an attempt to forget the horrors they had been through. Gradually, the culture of motorcycling began to develop into an alternative lifestyle, with movies like *The Wild One*, which was produced in 1953, and starred Marlon Brando, influencing many people's perceptions. This epic was followed two years later by *Rebel Without A Cause*, with James Dean in the lead role. The media quickly seized on the opportunity to paint bikers as the bad guys—a situation that has lasted until the present day.

Many of the ex-military machines that were turned over to civilian use were initially stripped of unnecessary things like their fenders to make them both lighter and easier to work on. Before long, this led to changes being made purely for style reasons, and customising began to take off as an art form. The most popular type of custom was what became known as the "Chopper." This name arose because the bikes had been "chopped and dropped." Performance was seen as a secondary factor to looks, and long forks, low seats, fancy paint and loud pipes ruled the day.

These days, motorcycle customisation has grown into a major industry, but in its early years there were no suppliers of specialist parts. Builders had a stark choice—they could make their own from scratch, they could modify stock components, or they could contract a local fabricator to do the job for them. Consequently, many of the bikes that were built were not roadworthy, and many accidents occurred. It was not long, however, before the gap in the market was seen and filled by various outfits who advertised their products in the motorcycle press. A lot of these parts were badly made, but over time the word spread and these companies went under. A few others, however, gained an excellent reputation for quality—a number of these used the drag-strip as a test bed. S&S Cycle, for instance, started making engine components for Harley-Davidsons in 1958, and quickly became the preferred suppliers to many of the top racers of the day. Ever since their humble beginnings, they have continued to grow, and today, they are one of the leading manufacturers of performance parts.

In the 1970s, several magazines sprang up which specialised in custom bikes, with titles like *Easyriders* and *Iron Horse* leading the way. These featured the best bikes around, and before long it seemed that people were building chops and lowriders right across the world. In recent years, the subject has received an enormous amount of media attention thanks to televised series such as those which put the spotlight on companies like Orange County Choppers. These days the amount of money and effort that is required to take a place at a top show means that the home-builder needs to demonstrate the very highest levels of craftsmanship if he has a chance of competing.

LEFT: The greatest movie in motorcycling history has to be *Easy Rider*, which first aired in 1969. It starred Peter Fonda and Dennis Hopper, and had a massive influence on the custom bike movement. The scene shown here was probably filmed in Louisiana. *Bettmann/Corbis U1636710B*

**ABOVE:** These days you no longer have to build your own custom bike—you can simply walk into a store and buy a new one, just like any other motorcycle. *Keith Syvinski*

**ABOVE:** Owner Paul Funk built this bike as a showcase for his PTP engine. The main inspiration behind his design was that he wanted to build something that was true to the Harley heritage, but at the same time was constructed using 21st century engineering.
*Paul Funk*

LEFT: This bike has been built with weight and performance in mind—the nitrous oxide bottle is not there merely for show! *Paul Funk*

**LEFT:** The sign of a properly-built machine is a thorough attention to detail. *Paul Funk*

**ABOVE:** Once a bike has been finished, the best place for it is out on the road . . . *Paul Funk*

**PAGE 116:** This chop, seen at the Dirt Bag Rally in San Francisco 2007, was built by pro skateboarder Max Schaff. He is a keen biker, and performed all the fabrication himself. *Max Schaff*

**PAGE 117:** Max's custom bike uses a Knucklehead engine in a hardtail frame. The unusual exhausts were home-made. *Max Schaff*

PAGES **118–122:** This custom bike-entitled "Captain America" was built as a homage to the machine which starred in the film *Easy Rider*. It is not an exact replica—it has the wrong engine, for a start, but is no less special for that. *Simon Clay*

LIVE LIFE FULL THROTTLE
#068 OF 750
CMC
USA
CAPTAIN AMERICA

LEFT: This "Retro board track racer" epitomises tasteful design—it is simple, clean, and above all, superbly-executed. *Simon Clay*

BELOW LEFT: Disc brakes are a modern feature, and yet they don't look out of place on this lovely machine. *Simon Clay*

BELOW: The rocker covers on the Shovelhead engine have been engraved with the words "Milwaukee Iron, Made In America." *Simon Clay*

**ABOVE:** This Evolution-engined custom bike features all manner of special parts, ranging from billet wheels and swing-arm to Performance Machine brakes, and, of course, the lurid paintjob. *Simon Clay*

**RIGHT:** A V-Rod custom on show at the Harley Day in Arnhem, Holland. *Henry Azuil*

**FAR LEFT:** Custom bikes come in many shapes, sizes and colors. This chop, with its striking yellow paint scheme has a telescopic front end and a Softail-style swing arm at the rear. *Keith Syvinski*

**LEFT:** Advances in modern tyre construction technologies have resulted in super-wide rubber becoming available to the custom bike market. *Keith Syvinski*

Show Vehicle - NOT FOR SALE

RIGHT: Whether one considers this to be a motorcycle or a car matters not—it show just what can be achieved with the resources of a large car company's design department. Called the Dodge Tomahawk, it was built as a concept vehicle by the Chrysler Group, and features a 500-horsepower Viper V-10 engine and four wheels. It was first shown at the 2003 North American International Auto Show. *Jason Boutsayaphat*

TOURERS
& DRESSERS

# TOURERS & DRESSERS

The large capacity V-twin motorcycle engine lends itself to a number of different uses. It has been highly successful, for instance, as the powerplant in many record-winning drag bikes. It is, however, perhaps most at home when used as the heart of the long-distance touring bike. The roads of the United States lend themselves to such machines, with low, and often heavily-enforced speed limits, combined with huge mileages. In these circumstances, reliability and low rider fatigue are the most important considerations, and on this front the big V-twin excels. In order to cater to the varied tastes of such owners, Harley-Davidson produce a wide range of touring models. Most tend to be personalized to some extent—those which carry a lot of extras are generally known as "dressers."

LEFT: This Police Special is powered by the Twin Cam Evolution engine—it is basically a Road Glide tourer that has been fitted with extra equipment to make it more suitable for law enforcement purposes. *Simon Clay*

ABOVE: The Road King—designated as the FLHR—replaced the Electra-Glide in 1994. It has a five gallon fuel capacity and both panniers and windshield have been designed to be easily removed. *Simon Clay*

FAR LEFT: This dresser features a highly unusual paintjob, which lists the names of soldiers who were recorded as POW (prisoners of war) or MIA (missing in action) during the Vietnam conflict. *Simon Clay*

THESE PAGES: The Electra-Glide Ultra Classic was produced as a 90th Anniversary Limited Edition model. It featured a number of unusual accessories, including a cruise-control system. *Simon Clay*

LEFT: Left-hand side view of the Electra-Glide Ultra Classic 90th Anniversary Limited Edition model. *Simon Clay*

ABOVE AND ABOVE RIGHT: This Road King dresser, with its windshield, panniers, and extra lights is well-equipped for long distance work. *Simon Clay*

RIGHT: This Evolution-engined dresser is based around the Springer Softail, but with the addition of such things as a windshield and saddlebags. *Simon Clay*

**LEFT:** This Springer Softail FXSTS has been personalized with a special flame paintjob that would normally be considered more at home on a chop. *Simon Clay*

**BELOW LEFT:** Most of the instruments on the Springer Softail FXSTS are mounted in a console on the gas tank. This model sold extremely well, and demand was such that the second year's production run was four times greater than first expected. *Simon Clay*

**BELOW:** The Electra-Glide Ultra has a well-equipped dashboard, with a large number of instruments, as well as a stereo and, in some cases, a CB radio. *Simon Clay*

# MILITARY BIKES

**ABOVE LEFT:** It was not long after motorcycles were first invented that they were first used for military purposes—the sidecar outfit seen here has been modified to carry a mount for a light machine gun. *Library of Congress*

**ABOVE:** This Indian sidecar outfit has been modified to act as a stretcher carrier—as the title says "Motor Cycle Ambulance-Hero Land." *Library of Congress*

**LEFT:** This early photograph shows the Military motor cycle squad lined up for inspection. *Library of Congress*

**PREVIOUS PAGE:** Following on from the success in desert conditions of German military motorcycles which had a low center of gravity combined with shaft final drive, the U.S. Army made an official request for experimental machines along similar lines. In 1942, in response to this requirement, the Harley-Davidson company produced the machine shown here. It was designated as the "XA," which stood for "Experimental Army." *Tria Giovan/Corbis*

# MILITARY BIKES

The U.S. Army had experimented with using motorcycles for such purposes as communication since their first appearance, but it was not until the punitive expeditions against Pancho Villa in 1916 that they were used in action. When the United States entered World War I in 1917, the U.S. Army bought almost a third of the year's entire production of Harley-Davidsons: in total, it would purchased about some 20,000.

In the late 1930s, the rise of Nazi Germany put the world on a war footing once again. The U.S. Army knew that it was likely to see fighting and so began preparing for action. President Roosevelt tried to keep the U.S. out of it as he had been elected on the promise that he would not send American troops into battle, but when Japan attacked Pearl Harbor in 1941, he was left with little choice. The first ground troops arrived in England in January 1942, some of whom were equipped with motorcycles such as the Harley-Davidson WLA and Indian Chiefs, Scouts, or Junior Scouts. The WLA was essentially a civilian machine with a low-powered side-valve engine that had been converted for military use. The modifications included such things as olive drab paint, no chrome or nickel plating, special lights that could be used under blackout conditions, improved air filtration and racks for carrying special equipment such as machine-guns, radios,

**ABOVE:** *Troy Sherk*

**BELOW:** Official photo, State Historical Society, Sanitary Co., Fourth Nebraska National Guard. c1917. *Library of Congress*

etc. In order to reduce the likelihood of the fenders becoming jammed with mud, the sides were removed—the exact specification varied, however, depending on the machine's specific use.

One of the U.S. Army's main concerns with regard to its motorcycles was how well they would cope with desert conditions. German bikes such as the BMWs had demonstrated that a low center of gravity combined with shaft final drive gave a superior performance in deep sand. As a consequence of this, there was an official request for experimental machines along similar lines. Harley-Davidson responded with a machine that was designated the XA—this was fitted with a flat-twin boxer engine with a similar layout to that of the BMW. Indian came up with the 841, an across the frame V-twin with plunger rear suspension. Both had shaft drive in order to eliminate the problems associated with using drive chains in off-road conditions. Some Harley-Davidson big-twins were used by the military, although these were mostly used for escort work as they were too heavy for use on rough terrain. When the war ended, vast numbers of these bikes were broken up for scrap, and most of the others were modified for use by civilian riders. Consequently, few original examples are left, and they are now highly sought-after by collectors.

POLICE BIKES

PREVIOUS PAGE: A line up of police department motorcyclists—some are solo machines, whereas those nearest the camera are sidecar outfits. *Dudley Perkins Family*

THIS PAGE: Motorcycle cops. 1922. *Library of Congress*

# POLICE BIKES

There is a long history of American motorcycles being used by law enforcement agencies the world over. In the early days, a wide variety of makes were employed, however, as time went on most of the manufacturers fell by the wayside. In the end, only Harley-Davidson were left, however, the rise of the Japanese import trade soon put the company under intense pressure. Things got much worse during the period of AMF ownership, and many police departments were unwilling to continue using machines that they felt were over-priced and, in many cases, very unreliable. As a consequence of this, many Shovelhead-engined bikes were sold off and significant numbers of motorcycles made by rivals such as Honda and Kawasaki were bought to replace them. Fortunately, Harley-Davidson's return to private ownership saw the release of the Evolution engine in 1984, and with this came a massive upturn in the factory's reputation. These days, Harleys are once again the machine of choice for many leading forces.

TOP LEFT: Police guard beside his motorcycle, near the White House. *Library of Congress*

TOP CENTER: Police guards with motorcycles near the White House. *Library of Congress*

TOP RIGHT: Boulder Police department motorcyclists wait at the side of the road on their Twin-Cam Evolution-engined machines. *Joel Terrell*

RIGHT: This Michigan State Police bike, which is powered by an Evolution engine, came equipped with the fairing and hard luggage cases as standard. *Simon Clay*

THIS PAGE: A line up of seven police department motorcycles and their riders around the year 1920. *Dudley Perkins Family*

**LEFT AND ABOVE:** Motorcycle police trailing a
car belching smoke. September 1, 1923.
*Library of Congress*

# UTILITY BIKES
# & OUTFITS

# UTILITY BIKES & OUTFITS

These days the vast majority of American motorcycles are used for pleasure, rather than for commercial reasons. This was not always the case, however, and for most of the twentieth century, a large proportion had to earn a living as workhorses of one kind or another. Some were specially-constructed to provide extra carrying capacity—this often involved the fitment of a sidecar. Machines thus equipped were a viable alternative to automobiles like the Ford Model T. One of the best-known American-produced utility vehicles was the Servi-Car.

**LEFT:** Mr and Mrs Willie Kay on their Indian Tricar in an advertisement for "Indian Motorcycle and Tri-cars." Mrs Kay is sitting in a seat fitted between the front wheels while her husband peddles the 3-wheeled motor bicycle. c.1906. *Library of Congress*

**ABOVE:** A commercial Harley-Davidson sidecar outfit, complete with slogans advertising the Dudley Perkins dealership was probably taken around 1918. *Dudley Perkins Family*

**FAR LEFT:** This photo will probably shock many people in our overly-sensitised society, however, when it was taken sometime around 1920, hunting was still seen as an acceptable pastime to the majority of the public. *Dudley Perkins Family*

**LEFT:** Jimmy Murphy, winner of the 500-mile auto race at Indianapolis, Indiana, May 30, 1922. He is accompanied by his mechanic, Ernie Olson, who is seated in the sidecar of the Harley-Davidson motorcycle. c. June, 1922 . *Library of Congress*

**BELOW:** At the 1931 Minnesota State Fair, the Guy Webb motorcycle shop exhibits several models of its specialty, Harley-Davidson motorcycles. *Minnesota Historical Society/Corbis*

**RIGHT:** This Indian sidecar outfit has been brought up to date with a few modern parts—they are all appropriate though, and the finished product is a machine to be proud of. *Jim Service*

**ABOVE:** In an attempt to provide a rival to the hordes of Italian scooters which were being sold in the post-war era, Harley-Davidson began work on their own interpretation of what such a vehicle should look like. In 1960, they released the Topper motor scooter; sadly, it was a sales disaster, and after a run of five years was discontinued. This example is from the collection of the Dudley Perkins Company. *Randy Dodson/Dudley Perkins Family*

**RIGHT:** The M65 was another attempt by the Harley-Davidson company to produce a motorcycle that could rival the cheap imports from Europe and Japan. It was essentially a re-badged Italian two-stroke, but by the time it had been released, however, it was behind the times, and was not a sales success. This example, from 1966, is from the collection of Jack Christianson. *Randy Dodson/Dudley Perkins Family*

# INDEX